Black Scientists of America

Richard X. Donovan

National Book Company
Portland, Oregon

ED-R

Illustrations   Judith Sorrels

297000

0-89420-265-0

Contents

Chapter 1

The Many and The Few

Chapter 1

The Many and The Few

At the Library of Congress in Washington, D.C., a "Who's Who of Black Scientists" is being prepared by a dedicated lady, on her own time. She estimates that upon completion, the volume will include about 1500 names. There are, of course, many more Black scientists; but if 1500 is a fraction of the total, it is a respectable figure, which puts to rest the unknowing question "Are there Black scientists?"

The "Who's Who" is therefore a labor of love and logic, and will be useful to Blacks and others as a means of communicating, and sharing information and purpose. And the young may be motivated to think ahead to a day when they might be included in some future edition of that book.

It has been said that most of the scientists who ever lived are alive today. The revolution in science, which began with the Renaissance, went into high gear in the 20th Century. Science has never been more peopled and professional than it is today. As information and knowledge multiply, science becomes more and more specialized. And as more fields are created, more opportunities arise and more entrants are attracted.

It is fair to say, therefore, that most of the Black scientists who ever lived are alive today. This is a reflection of the general trend, but also a reflection of greater opportunity. Among many other factors, a debt is owed to the pioneers of Black scientific endeavor. As encouraging as this trend is, it must be noted that Black scientists, as a proportion of all American scientists, are very much under-represented. Standing alone, 1500 is a respectable figure. Measured against the total, it suggests that much progress is needed.

And while this "Who's Who" is exhaustive in its research into Black scientific leaders, it is primarily a research tool; you cannot *read* it conveniently. *Black Scientists of America* makes no attempt to identify every Black scientist, but simply tries to explain a little more detail about the lives of a few of particular accomplishment, and frame their contributions in a narrative that all can more easily appreciate.

This book deals mainly with what was and what is. What could be is for the young readers of these words to imagine . . . and bring to reality. The future is imponderable; but there is reason for optimism, in the sense that a promising trend will not be reversed. The question is: How fast will the pace be?

Black scientists alive today have advantages the likes of which past generations of scientists would not have dreamed. And young Black scientists and students have significant advantages over those of their elders in science. The quality of education and training, the facilities, financial support, and number of internships — all are very much higher, and very much more available.

It is fair to say that while opportunities for Black scientists trail behind the norm, they also have never been greater. Closing the gap is the challenge.

It is the kind of gap that knowledge helps to close. When there is something difficult to be done, it helps to know that someone has done it before you, when the task was even harder.

Few aspiring Black scientists today go to work in tobacco fields to finance their education. Few have an opportunity to become familiar with biology, botany, architecture, agronomy, journalism, medicine, and electrical engineering before making a career choice. If Benjamin Banneker could not do today, what he did in the 18th Century, it is also true that few in the present day could be a Benjamin Banneker. Most of life is trade-offs. The advantages open to Black scientists in the late 20th Century are incomparably better than in days gone by. Something may be lost in the process, but the net gain cannot be disputed.

Life is very much what we choose to emphasize. It is easy for some to emphasize the difficulties and the obstacles. Others may emphasize the opportunity and the challenge. Success is almost beyond reach unless a person emphasizes opportunity. Although chance cannot be ignored, it is primarily a matter of choice. In a way, though, we often choose the way we deal with chance. The key is to try, or opportunities and challenges go begging.

To try can lead to disappointment, but it may not. If we do not try, the game is over because it never began. Black scientists, and Black students of science, have never had more attractive opportunities and have never had more manageable challenges. There is a tide running that is unlikely to be — will not be allowed to be — reversed.

Chapter 2

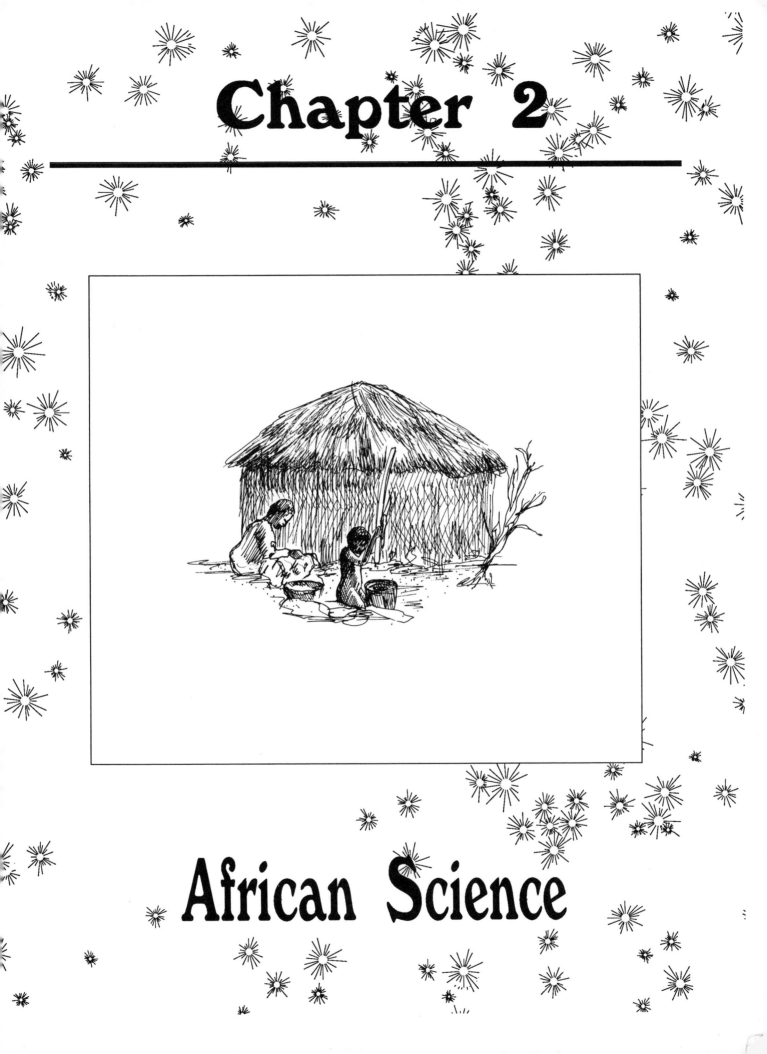

African Science

Chapter 2

African Science

What is science, in simple terms? It is an inquiry into nature, curiosity about why and how the world works as it does. Using this definition, almost all of us have been scientific at some time. Those who become expert are those who inquire into nature systematically and with skill, perhaps learning during this process, how to make nature work for them.

Science has flourished in different places and times around the world. It has also been especially varied in different times and places.

If the tide started its run ever so gradually in America, it did not run so gradually in Africa. Centuries before America was discovered, and while Europe awaited the Dark Ages, science in Africa was rich and dynamic.

We know enough of science in ancient Africa to know that it was striking both in its discoveries and the *application* of those discoveries. In Africa, in centuries past, achievements were notable in mathematics and astronomy.

Three hundred years before Christ, a complex astronomical observatory existed in Kenya. One result was a complex and accurate calendar system. During the same general period, the ancient Romans, preoccupied with conquest, were keeping track of time by pounding nails into a pole.

What were the conditions that led Africans in Kenya to develop a sophisticated system of astronomy while the Romans were pounding poles? We may as well ask what motivated George Washington Carver, alone at age 13, to persist in the quest for a higher education — we don't know the answer to either. Perhaps, however, some future Black historian or anthropologist might seek the answer to one or both questions.

African excellence in astronomy was evident not only in Kenya, but across the breadth of East Africa. All of this occurred in the first millennium before Christ, and a little later, emerged in the area that is now Mali.

Expert astronomy requires excellent mathematics. Number systems have been discovered in the Congo which date back 8000 years. These systems were among the first in the world and demonstrated a strong capability for logic and abstract thought.

African Science

Science flourishes especially when there is a need. Commerce in ancient Africa created the need for mathematics. It developed in Europe too; but there, and for a long time, numbers were met with suspicion. Mathematics was magic and superstition.

It is therefore unreasonable to say of Black students in America today that they cannot learn math. It does not help to hear: "It is hard, and most of you won't learn much, but it is a part of the school program, and we have to take it even though we don't like it." Students of all races hear this, but the initiatives of Black students may be especially inhibited by the condescension.

Just as mathematics flourished in Africa long ago, it can flourish among Black students today — with the right encouragement. A single volume, published in 1980, contains the work of sixty-two distinguished Black mathematicians.

Astronomy and mathematics were the outstanding sciences in Ancient Africa, but there were others. Shipbuilding was an African talent, and shipbuilding required mathematics, physics, and engineering. The ancient Chinese record the coming of Africans to the court of China in excellent sailing ships. As early as the 13th Century,

Africans brought elephants to China. This was 200 years *before* Columbus sailed to America.

Africans also used navigational science to cross the Sahara. Such a journey is *twice* as long and more dangerous than the sea voyage to America.

The scientific achievements of Africa accumulate: astronomy, mathematics, physics, engineering, nautical, and navigational sciences.

Agricultural sciences were also strong. It is very interesting that African-cultivated cotton appears to have intermarried with American wild cotton as early as 3500 B.C. It seems unlikely that this happened accidentally. In addition to the Scandinavians, did the Africans come to the New World long before Columbus?

All through history, the domestication of cattle has been a key indicator of civilization. Africans may have domesticated cattle as early as 15,000 years ago. And grains were used domestically as early as 6000 years ago.

It is unclear how this early excellence in science may have affected the rest of the world. But Africans were seafarers, and it is reasonable that they spread their knowledge afar, perhaps to the Western World, across the Mediterranean.

African herbal medicine was advanced, too, and even in modern times, herbal medicine is used there in the treatment of psychosis. Surgical skills were also keen. Antiseptic surgery and Caesarian deliveries were skillfully done in Africa, long before they were common in Europe.

Even those more primitive practitioners who came to be called "witch doctors" were often successful because they understood both the local herbs and the power of suggestion. Medication and suggestion are two of the keystones of modern psychotherapy.

And so, at a time when Europe was still undefined, African science knew areas of excellence.

But the earliest Blacks in science are a distant encouragement to Blacks today, who have more recent examples of those who cleared a hurdle.

One of those examples we will discuss next. He is a transition, over the centuries, from the days of African astronomy and mathematics, to today's books full of learned papers by Black mathematicians.

Chapter 3

Transition in the New World

Chapter 3

Transition in the New World

Benjamin Banneker could not happen today. Neither could Thomas Edison nor Henry Ford, nor rocket pioneer Robert Goddard. Something is lost and something is gained. There is still ample opportunity for today's individual scientist, but it is within a framework of which pioneers could not have dreamed. Banneker was one inquirer who only casually interacted with the few congenial men around him. For the most part, he did it on his own.

How much of Banneker's achievements should we assign to natural endowments, and how much to environment? It's a puzzle. We can safely say: "Some of both," without assigning percentages. Environment is what we know best.

Benjamin Banneker was the first Black American scientist that we know of. He lived from 1731 to 1806. In early childhood, there occurred one of those accidents or imponderables which have consequences that can't be measured. His grandmother taught him to read, so that he in turn could read the Bible to her. The happy chance was that his grandmother, born in the 17th Century, could read. It is a further wonder that she was present to teach Benjamin, and then to provide occasions for him to read quite naturally at an early, pre-school age.

We should note that there are examples, in the lives of other Black scientists, of the most normal occurrences or accidents that nevertheless changed their lives.

Banneker had the immense additional advantage of being free. This meant that he had time and energy to devote to study and experimentation. He might easily have been a slave, condemned to the drudgery of the fields.

At an early age, Banneker showed interest in all things mechanical. Later in his life, mechanical skill would be a positive genius.

Free as he was, he was able to attend an integrated school where he received the equivalent of an eighth grade education. Measured against the standards of those times, this was a notable accomplishment.

Transition in the New World

What was possible then — and improbable now — was the extension of an eighth grade education by individual effort. Banneker's skill in mathematics seemed to come from nowhere. He needed only rudimentary instruction in arithmetic from which to teach himself algebra and geometry.

Today, such things happen almost entirely in the classrooms of formal education. But for Banneker the classroom closed around age 14, and he was more or less on his own. Individual effort extends the classroom education, and he knew what to do, or, at least, what he wanted to learn more about. He taught himself — probably through trial and error — how to find the knowledge he sought. The freedom to *do* so itself was an incentive, and his talent served him well.

By the time he was a young adult, Banneker was the most learned person, Black or white, in his region. He was marked as an outstanding man. His response was modest, but there was the disadvantage that he had no peers. There was no one to talk to and very little external stimulus. In one of those imponderable accidents which mark many lives, this was to change.

In 1772, when Banneker was 41, there arrived in his valley a family named the Ellicotts. The father, George, a learned and curious man himself, became his close friend and their conversations were rich in sharing and mutual interest.

There were also economic advantages which were very welcome. But unlike other free Blacks, Banneker refused to own slaves, although financially he would have benefitted greatly. His character and his convictions were as strong as his intellectual capacity.

One of his talents was writing math problems in verse. His verses were much in demand among the aristocracy of the region, and the poetic puzzles were awaited with zest. "Literary mathematics" is rare. Banneker's skill is a testament to his verbal as well as his non-verbal accomplishments.

After seeing an imported clock in the 1750s, Banneker devoted the years 1758 to 1761 to building a clock of his own. He succeeded, and the first completely American clock was the result. The clock won him notice far and wide, and people travelled to him for a demonstration of its workings. Later, on the day of his funeral, the clock and most of Banneker's notes were destroyed when his home burned down. Somehow, much later, the clock was reconstructed by others. The replica is in existence.

His mind was so agile and forward-looking that when his friend, George Ellicott, loaned him astronomy books and instruments, he quickly pointed out errors in the texts, and took their knowledge a step further.

He grasped so quickly that he leapt forward naturally, and was immediately extending his knowledge to a point that was beyond the grasp of most others. He was a self-made man, with all the right ingredients.

Because he understood things so well, he began in 1791 to publish his own almanac. Among other things, he calculated the cycle of the 17-year plague of locusts.

He also used his almanac for political purposes. He urged freedom for the slaves, he suggested a "Peace Office" for the United States, and he foresaw the U.S. Department of the Interior and the United Nations. He could apply his mind to verbal and non-verbal purposes with almost equal ease, as shown in his "poetic math."

A memorable and singular contribution to the nation came when he was called upon by the President of the United States to assist in planning the new capital of Washington, D.C.

At a critical point in the work, the Frenchman L'Enfant, the project leader, became dissatisfied. Bitterly and abruptly he seized all the plans and returned with them to France. The feeling among those left behind was that all was lost. But Banneker stepped in with his prodigious memory and turned despair into success. He reproduced the plans from memory, almost without flaw. The nation is in his debt. The present-day layout of the National Capital would not be possible without his remarkable talents.

As our nation entered the 19th Century, Banneker was 69 and in what was to be the twilight of his singular life. He was used to a daily walk in the woods near his home. One day in 1806, he walked into the woods and collapsed. He died soon after.

It was said that Benjamin Banneker could not happen today. That is both a tribute to him and a tribute to the progress of science since his death. It does not follow that he would have been a misfit today. With his endowments and his talent for leap-frogging knowledge, and the training which is now available, he would most likely have been preeminent in astronomy or mathematics. He might have won or shared a Nobel Prize.

Most certainly, his education would not have stopped after the eighth grade.

But there is still something especially noble about his accomplishments. It is true of other pioneers of science. What was possible then is impossible now. And that represents both progress and regret. Something's lost, and something's gained.

If we knew more about Banneker's life, we could better assess what followed. As it is, we can readily identify native talent, freedom, and a good education for his day. For years, he provided his own stimulus. Later, the coming of his neighbor, George Ellicott, made possible the exchange of stimulus with a peer. Over 100 years before the Emancipation Proclamation, he enjoyed the closest and most rewarding friendship with an accomplished white.

Banneker's political involvements had been moderate but persistent. Toward the end of his life, and during the presidency of Thomas Jefferson, Banneker wrote to Jefferson, urging better treatment for the slaves. We do not know if Jefferson and Banneker knew each other personally; but Jefferson surely knew Banneker's reputation, and respected it greatly.

Jefferson replied to Banneker's letter promptly. He praised Banneker's "moral eminence" and regretted the "degraded condition" in which most Blacks were kept. Jefferson's thoughts on slavery grew more progressive as he became older; and yet he gave no recognition to the influence of freedom on Banneker's life of accomplishment. Perhaps it did not even occur to him.

Freedom, education, and encouragement from somewhere — these are recurring elements in the stories of Black scientists. Benjamin Banneker was unique, but so were others.

Chapter 4

Equal to the Task

Chapter 4

Equal to the Task

A famous man is remembered for his accomplishments; but also because the record of his life was preserved and handed down, in writing or by word of mouth. There are countless men and women of accomplishment who are not remembered because they were seldom publicized. And there are times when just a little information makes us wish we knew much more.

An example is *Daniel A. Payne*, a free man in the days of slavery. We know that he received an education that was thorough, for his day. From somewhere, at some age, must have come encouragement. We do not know whether it was from parents, a teacher, or a chance encounter with nature. We do know that for some gifted persons, it takes only the briefest experience to light a spark that lasts a lifetime.

Payne, like Banneker, used his formal schooling not as an ending but as a point of departure. On his own, he taught himself Greek, Latin, French, botany, and zoology. He became expert in zoology by catching and dissecting his own animals.

Again, something is lost and something is gained. Today's zoology is taught under superior classroom and laboratory conditions, where a variety of animals are available for examination. Knowledge has expanded enormously and instruction is experienced and stimulating. But something is lost when the ways of the pioneers are lost, when catching and dissecting animals all alone would now be very difficult and probably illegal.

Science, as an inquiry into nature, goes on. If once there was the free inquiry of an individual, today the lines of inquiry are very much more elaborate and exciting. Neither Banneker, Payne, nor Ben Franklin ever had the secure standing of a professional. But because they came first, the building of a profession was possible. Lone investigators gradually banded together.

It is likely that the pioneer combination of science and the humanities is also a fading condition. The mass of information, even within a single scientific specialty, is such that it requires all of one's professional attention. So much so, that specialties are continually subdividing, generating more and more knowledge in a narrower focus.

Daniel Hale Williams was born in 1856. His father died when he was 11, and his mother deserted him, after apprenticing him to a cobbler. By all odds, that should have been the end of it. For all intents and purposes, he was orphaned before his teens, and imprisoned in a trade that appeared to have no exit.

But Williams also took a part-time job as a barber, and choice and chance came together. When this happens, it is well to let the two cooperate. He did.

One of his barbershop customers was a medical doctor who talked to him about medicine. It could have gone in one ear and out the other. It could have bored or confused him. Instead, it inspired him.

But that was not enough. Williams had to *act*. For two years, Williams apprenticed with the doctor.

Apprenticing, as practiced in years gone by, is no longer acceptable. But it served many people well, as men like Abraham Lincoln would attest.

Williams' two years of medical apprenticeship convinced him that medicine was his life. We do not know how it was done financially, but he entered the Chicago Medical College and came out a doctor. He was true to himself.

Once a doctor, Williams was heard from. He became troubled and disturbed by the prevailing discrimination against Black medical professionals, and he made a choice. He opened his own medical hospital as a haven for Black doctors and nurses and as a place where they could gain practical experience.

This step was a logical and successful innovation in a situation where there was no promising alternative. Once again, Williams had seized an opportunity and produced a constructive result.

But later, and quite by chance, he made the choice for which he is best remembered. In 1893, when Williams was 37, a knifing victim was brought to his hospital, with a wound in his heart. The condition of the patient was such that time was of the essence.

Williams made a decision; and under the most difficult conditions, he performed the first open heart surgery. He did this without X-rays, without blood for transfusion, and without anesthesia.

The operation was efficient and successful. The patient lived on for 20 years. But there was a national uproar, because of the radical and trail-blazing nature of the surgery, and because the surgeon was Black.

Fame comes naturally to the one who is first. From a bleak future as a cobbler's apprentice, choice and chance combined to make Daniel Hale Williams outstanding. There is no evidence that he sought fame, in an under-equipped hospital that he had set up as a medical refuge for Black doctors and nurses. True to his own convictions, he studied and worked to achieve his own goals. Confirming his choices and efforts, fame came to him.

Death and desertion were his early lot; and there is little in such origins to suggest a successful professional future. But there was something there to blossom when the occasion arose.

By the time Williams was practicing medicine, it was a profession in almost every sense of the word. Formal education and structure had replaced apprenticeship, some of which still survives in the form of internship.

What is encouraging is that within all of this new structure, it was (and remains) possible for a single person to innovate impressively. He or she cannot do it with the independence of a Banneker, but within the system, "firsts" are still there to be pursued.

Noteworthy firsts for Black scientists include these additional achievements. The first Black doctor we know of was *James Derham*, born in 1762. He was apprenticed, won his freedom, and set up his own practice in New Orleans.

The first Black dentistry graduate was *Robert Tanner Freeman*, who graduated from Harvard University in 1867.

In 1876, the first Ph.D was conferred on a Black. The degree was granted, in physics, to *Edward Bouchet*, by Yale University.

In 1925, Cornell University conferred the first Ph.D in pure mathematics ever to be granted to a Black American. The recipient was *Elbert Frank Cox*.

Yale University, in 1949, granted the first Ph.D in mathematics to a Black woman — *Evelyn Boyd Glanville*.

The first Black woman doctor was *Susan McKinney*, who graduated from New York Medical College in 1870.

The first Black professor at Harvard was *Dr. William A. Hinton*, in the Medical School (1949).

If it is now difficult to be the lone innovator, it is still possible to be first. And it is probably easier. Consider the difficulties of Black science students who aspired to the Ph.D degree a mere decade after the Emancipation Proclamation. Trails have been blazed, though still others lie ahead.

To gain entrance into a prestigious Ivy League university was a victory in itself.

There had to be encouragement, education, financial support, good choices, and the right chances. None of these eliminate the built-in difficulty in being the first Black in any branch of science. But the trend is right.

Equal to the Task

By the 20th Century, enough trails had been blazed to make the entry of Blacks into science easier, if not easy.

What marks 20th Century Black scientists also marks scientists as a whole. The distinguishing mark is greater professionalism.

Dr. Charles R. Drew is remembered well, even today, for pioneering the development of blood preservation research and blood banks.

Drew's accomplishments were predictable early in his career. When he graduated from Amherst, he was recognized as the student who had brought the most honor to the school during his four years.

He introduced blood plasma to the battlefield in World War II and in a single stroke saved far more lives (indeed thousands more) than he ever could have saved in the normal practice of medicine. As is the way with research in medicine or other fields, the discoveries of research can have broad application, while the researcher or research team remain little known. Happily, this anonymity is sometimes overcome when the Nobel Prizes are conferred.

Drew was also responsible for the establishment of the American Red Cross blood bank, which serves the entire nation in time of need, whether it be an individual need or a more general disaster. He served as head of the

Howard University surgery department, and as chief surgeon at Freedman's Hospital, Washington, D.C.

It was while taking a group of science students to a meeting in 1950 that he had the tragic auto accident which claimed his life. He died in the service of others.

Drew's scientific gifts to humanity can be measured in countless lives saved. He blazed trails, after first choosing an initial trail for himself.

Dr. Charles F. Whitten is a medical doctor, who has specialized in the causes and cure of sickle cell anemia. His family tradition was expressed in ". . . bettering yourself through education." He took this to heart and at age 6 he was determined to be a doctor. This determination survived his father's death when he was 10, and was reinforced by his mother's heroism in keeping the family together.

He became president of the National Association for Sickle Cell Disease. He also served as Professor of Pediatrics at the Wayne State University Medical School.

Black scientists have made precise and important contributions to the space program and to the resulting understanding of our own planet. *George E. Carruthers*, born in 1940 and the holder of a doctorate in physics, came from Chicago's South Side. At the young age of 22, he was one of two who were responsible for placing on the moon a special camera and spectrograph. For the first time, photographs were obtained of the ultraviolet bands of atomic oxygen around the equator. Because of this contribution to our understanding of planet Earth, Carruthers received NASA's Exceptional Scientific Achievement Medal.

Black scientists, successful though they have been, have not always been employed by others. Some have been outstanding entrepreneurs. *Dr. Percy Julian* opened his own pharmaceutical laboratory and made discoveries which led to mass production of drugs used in the treatment of arthritis and glaucoma. Once again, the beneficiaries of the research of a Black scientist numbered in the thousands, and, very probably, millions. Relief from pain and blindness are surely a priceless gift.

Daniel Hale Williams, whom we saluted as the pioneer of open heart surgery, had an assistant, *Dr. Ulysses Grant Dailey*, who lived from 1885 to 1961. Dailey graduated in 1906 from the Northwestern University Medical School, and eventually opened his own hospital in Chicago.

He was very much a man of the 20th Century and his name became linked with astounding developments in surgery and anatomy. In 1933, he travelled worldwide under the sponsorship of the International College of Surgeons. In 1951, and again in 1953, the U.S. Department of State sent him to Asia and Africa as a much respected doctor and as a goodwill ambassador. Dr.

Dailey probably had more impact overseas, for medicine and for America, than any other Black scientist.

Dr. Ernest E. Just is a revered name in the history of Black scientists. He was a biologist who lived from 1883 to 1941. As a child, he moved with his mother from Charleston, South Carolina, to New York City, in search of better schools. Note the choice. At Dartmouth College, he was stimulated by a distinguished professor, and was the only *magna cum laude* graduate in his class. He was also Phi Beta Kappa.

His work on the life of cells and on egg fertilization was very advanced and therefore controversial. Many of his theories have stood the test of time; and he constantly refined them as more information became available.

For many years, Dr. Just was Professor of Zoology at Howard University, in Washington, D.C. His name is revered there, and a science building is named in his honored memory. He served as Vice President of the American Society of Zoologists.

Dr. Just was among other Black scientists whose family relocated for better educational advantages. The value placed on education has been a powerful spur. And so it is today, but opportunities are far more numerous. Relocation is more likely to mean a move within a metropolitan area than a move of hundreds of miles.

Equal to the Task

Dr. Leonidas H. Berry wrote the definitive text on endoscopy, or the examination of the interior of the human body. In doing so, he joined an elite group of Black scientists whose research gave life or relief to thousands.

His work helped to avert countless exploratory surgeries, saving lives in the process and sparing the trauma that is unavoidable in surgical procedures.

Dr. Albert C. Atoine, growing up in the toughest of Bronx neighborhoods, beat the odds with the inspiration of his parents. He literally studied his way out of his environment. His reward was a Ph.D and a useful life in research. His work on jet fuels has contributed significantly to aircraft performance and to the nation's efforts in outer space. These accomplishments may not carry the life-or-death implications of medical research, but their contribution to human progress is just as positive.

At the University of California, San Francisco, is the nation's largest kidney transplant and training program. It is the creation of *Dr. Samuel L. Kountz.* Dr. Kountz got there the hard way, and that very often pays off with the passage of time. He had to overcome many impediments to college entrance; but once there, he earned nothing but A's and B's. Now, his work on the drug treatment of kidneys has saved countless lives.

Repeatedly, we find Black scientists excelling in medical research, with the result that it is applied to patients in such numbers that honest gratification comes dramatically — even if less directly than for the practitioner.

Dr. Earl Shaw was the son of a sharecropper, who grew up with a steady confidence in his ability to become a laser physicist..

How such a goal emerged, and how it was sustained, we do not know. We do know that his uneducated mother struggled to teach him to read, and impressed upon him the value of a good education.

He believed that he received a fine primary education, from teachers who had no college degrees. Others seem to have felt the same. Primary school education was often solid and exciting, and more than sufficient motivation to go on, all the way to a Ph.D. Dr. Shaw did just that.

Many children of the ghetto went on to achieve lives of accomplishment. One of these was *Dr. Meredith Gourdine.* He was so intelligent and alert that his ghetto classes bored him, and he became a disruptive comedian. But into his life, at this point, came a teacher who challenged him to work to his potential.

He did, all the way to a Ph.D and beyond. Eventually, he solved a centuries-old problem by finding a way to convert gas to electricity, for practical uses.

Equal to the Task

Quite apart from his scientific successes, Dr. Gourdine was a broad-jumper in the 1952 Olympics.

Choice and chance are apparent once again. By chance the right teacher came along, and Dr. Gourdine made the choice to respond.

Dr. Archie Lacey was a recognized leader in science education.

Born in Alabama in 1923, he was the 13th of 16 children. He struggled for an education; and was forced to attend a segregated school, thirty-three miles from his home, with three white schools in between.

His sights seem to have been set early on science education. After graduating from college, he became a science instructor at a junior college, from 1949 to 1952.

He was motivated to pursue still higher education and earned a Master's degree and a Ph.D from Northwestern University, from 1953 to 1955. His doctorate was in education.

He became professor of physical sciences at Grambling College, from 1957 to 1960. A few years later he became the first Black male professor at Hunter College, in New York City. In 1969, he became a full professor at Lehman College, and in 1969, he set up the Department of Education at the new Federal City College in Washington, D.C.

Science education, like research in medicine, touches many thousands of people, often indirectly but nevertheless indelibly. Another example is *Dr. Warren Henry*, of Howard University, in Washington, D.C.

Dr. Henry is in his 81st year and is active on the physics faculty, after a distinguished career in government, industry, and education. The needs and interests of students are still his first concern.

As in the lives of many, a chance incident helped to mold his future. He was preparing for his senior year in high school and chanced to show his schedule to his mother. "What, no science?", she said. She produced her old science textbooks and as he looked at them, his interest in science awakened. A distinguished career was the result, and untold science students were the beneficiaries of a mother-son exchange.

Chapter 5

Standing Tall

Chapter 5

Standing Tall

"He could have added fortune to fame, but caring for neither, he found happiness and honor in being helpful to the world."

That is the epitaph of *George Washington Carver*. It was rare in its time, and would be even rarer today. It describes service without material gain, concern for others above self, and a praiseworthy sense of values in an age when values themselves are ridiculed by some.

Still he is remembered as perhaps the outstanding Black scientist, a pragmatist of inoffensive will, who became known for his quiet persuasion; and in the end, found his advice sought by the mighty.

His life is marked by events and decisions which are unusual. The man who resulted was singular.

George Washington Carver was born a slave in 1860, three years before Emancipation. He died in 1943, in the third term of Franklin D. Roosevelt.

As an infant, he was abducted from his owner's plantation, and was ransomed by his master, in exchange for a racehorse. It was a small, but very crucial bit of history.

The Civil War ended and soon after, at age 13, he was on his own. Consider a recent slave, venturing out into the turmoil of a postwar world, without any personal support and no material means — before normal maturity. He could have gone in many directions, good and bad. But he had the "right stuff," long before the term existed. He had one powerful goal — a high school education. It may seem a modest goal by modern standards; but for a Black youth, in the early 1870's, it was courageous.

He received his high school diploma, and then he raised his sights toward more education. After more than one rejection, he became the first Black student at Simpson College in Iowa, and then moved on to Iowa Agricultural College, which later became Iowa State University.

To support himself there, he worked as a janitor; but travelled the road of scholarship with persistence. In 1894, he received a Bachelor's degree in agricultural science, and two years later, a Master's degree.

In another step forward, Carver became the first Black faculty member at his alma mater. This attainment, recognizing his race, required a man who was far above the average.

Carver's teaching and research activities in Iowa began to make him well-known. Fame came his way, in spite of his reluctance to publish in the academic tradition.

His reputation reached as far as Booker T. Washington, the head of Tuskegee Institute in Alabama. Washington was not discouraged by Carver's failure to publish. He knew of him as an outstanding researcher, whose efforts had practical value. They were quite literally "down to earth" — Mother Earth.

In 1896, Washington offered Carver the position as head of the school's Agriculture Department, and he accepted. He returned from the Midwest to the Deep South, and the generally congenial atmosphere at Tuskegee. Oddly, for all of his practicality in agriculture, he was attacked by some as a "yankee" and an "ivory tower scientist."

None of this turned him aside. He focused immediately on the harm done to the South by the one-crop system, and had no illusions that threats to King Cotton would be handled without fireworks. He saw the need for new methods of scientific agriculture, tailor-made to the problems of the South.

Carver was not a politician; but he could persuade without offending, and when asked to present his case, he could deliver.

He pressed for the introduction of legumes — vegetables which did not deprive the soil of nitrates, as cotton did. At a time when fertilizer was scarce, his ideas made sense. He called for the planting of peas, soybeans, and peanuts.

Southern peanut growers had already banded together to promote their crop. Now they had an ally in Carver. They heard that "some old colored fella knew something about it;" and he was hustled in through the rear door of the hotel, where they were meeting. He stated his case and made a profound impression.

By 1921, Carver's reputation had spread to the U.S. Congress. There was the rare occurrence of a Southern-dominated House Ways and Means Committee inviting a Black man to come before it and give advice. He was allotted ten minutes to speak on Southern agriculture. When his *two hours* of testimony were finished, he received a standing ovation. He was not a politician; but his respectful confidence, and above all, his knowledge, had carried the day.

During his long career at Tuskegee, Carver received attractive job offers from many, including Thomas Edison and Henry Ford. He turned them all down. Money was the least of his interests. The epitaph that awaited him was accurate. His goal was to acquire and apply knowledge for the benefit of mankind. Tuskegee fitted him well in his pursuit of that goal. Tuskegee had sought him and he repaid the opportunity in a way that brought nothing but credit to the Institute. He not only turned down all outside offers, but he refused all royalties on his inventions.

Look in vain for his like today.

Carver saved the dying agriculture of the South, first by introducing the right combination of crops and then by finding and promoting markets for them. He was both the scientist and the entrepreneur; and he took nothing for his efforts, except his salary, from Tuskegee.

Carver died at the age of 83. He was active up to the very day of his death. He left to Tuskegee $33,000 — all he possessed.

The phrase "self-made man" applies to Carver, if it applies to anyone. We do not know from whence came his persistent forward motion, his persistence in presenting his views, or his skill in doing so without offending people who were set to oppose him. "He found happiness and honor." What an enviable treasure, and what a wonderfully satisfying discovery of life's deepest meaning. When the results were, and continue to be, so practical and beneficial, we are moved to remember him as a gently different man who made a giant difference.

Chapter 6

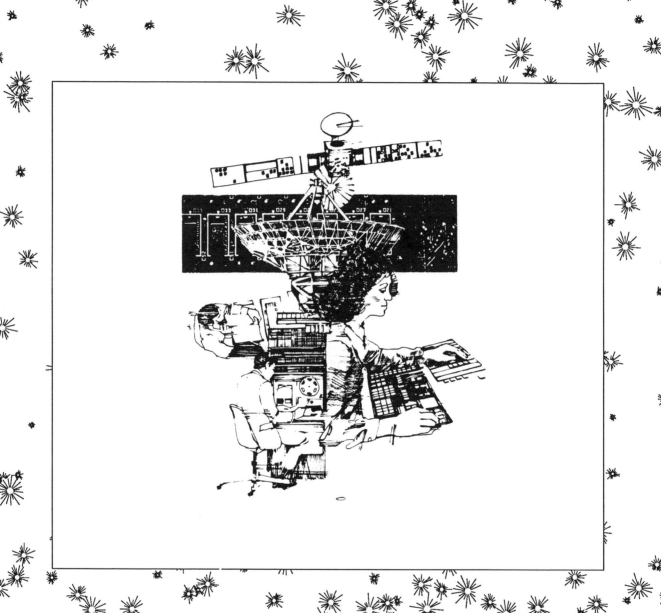

Black Women in Science

Chapter 6

Black Women in Science

Black women in science have cleared two hurdles — race and sex. The hurdles have been made a little easier with a combination of the civil rights movement and the feminist movement. Black women have thus availed themselves of a door that is a little more open. Energy, talent, and purpose are now more likely to prevail in any field, and not only in fields associated with science.

If Black women in science are less well known, there is still enough information to stimulate and encourage those who climb the ladder or are pondering which ladder to climb. It would be very helpful if more biographical data on Black women were available. As it is, the following gives glimpses of what is possible for those who aspire.

Jeanne Craig Sinkford was one of four daughters who worked out a "family plan" for higher education, where the older daughter gave financial support to the next youngest. They were strongly encouraged by their parents to do so. The two common elements appear again — education and encouragement.

When she was a junior in college, with the encouragement of her own family dentist, Jeanne Craig Sinkford set her sights on a career in dentistry. Having done so, she proceeded to graduate first in her dental school class at Howard University, in 1958. She continued on to obtain a doctorate in prosthodontics, which deals with dental crowns and bridgework.

In 1975, at Howard University, she became the first woman dental school dean in the United States; and she has continued to instruct.

Dr. Sinkford believes that a person should do what he or she likes to do. For those women in a position to follow that advice, she believes that dentistry is a perfect career, because of a woman's sense of esthetics and beauty, their compassion, and their small hands.

Dr. Sinkford, as a science administrator and educator, is in that group which we have already reviewed. They touch many for the future, both directly and indirectly, and in numbers that would not be possible in a one-on-one practice situation. Both are essential; but in our contacts with the individuals of science, it is well to remember the research, instruction, and information dissemination which stands behind them.

Dorothy Lavinia Brown, on the surface, does not fit the frequent pattern of "parental encouragement." From the age of 5 months to 12½ years, she was raised in an orphanage in Troy, N.Y. From somewhere, the spark was fanned. When she left the orphanage, education became a passion.

At age 14, she worked as a maid and laundress to support herself and to stay in school. She earned her B.A. degree from Bennett College, in 1941; and her M.D. from Meharry Medical College, in 1948.

She became the first Black woman surgeon in the South, and in 1957, she became chief of surgery at Riverside Hospital in Nashville. In 1965, she became clinical professor of surgery there.

In 1968, she was elected to the Tennessee legislature.

Is there better proof that it can be done? Dr. Brown, in her orphan origins, must have sensed that she was worth something. When she set out to prove it to herself, it was steady progress all the way to the very useful life of a surgeon and professor.

No one whose origins are humble should miss the lesson of an orphan's success, or of origins in the ghetto followed by a life of distinction. Often the path is easier, but when it is difficult, the record shows that it can be done — for indeed, it has been done.

Like Dr. Brown, *Dr. Jane C. Wright* was a surgeon and an educator. She graduated from Smith College in 1942, and went on to earn her M.D. from New York Medical College, in 1945. She succeeded her father as Director of the Harlem Hospital Cancer Research Foundation, and pioneered chemotherapy on tumors.

It is fascinating to see one lady proceed from an orphanage, while another followed in the footsteps of her prestigious father. Both emerged at approximately the same career position, and that is a credit to both of them. Count no one out. *Anything **is** possible.*

Although sources report all too little about her, we should mention the first Black woman doctor in the United States. She was *Susan McKinney*, and she graduated from the New York Medical College in 1870. This achievement, seven years after the Emancipation Proclamation, is so tantalizing that there is the wish to know more.

Life is often a matter of emphasis. One can say that the door to a career in science for Black women is half-open or half-closed. Since the door seems to be gradually opening somewhat more, perhaps that is where to put the emphasis.

Chapter 7

One Strong Life

Chapter 7

One Strong Life

Dr. Lafayette Frederick, Chairman of the Botany Department at Howard University, believes, lives, and teaches that nothing is beyond one's reach, if the effort is made.

In his own life, encouragement came early, principally from his parents, whose education was above average for the time. In so many instances, educated parents have made a difference. But just as important has been encouragement, whether the parents were highly educated or not. And frequently, encouragement took some tangible form, such as a change in locale to take advantage of better schools.

Dr. Frederick's parents were careful to encourage, in moral and practical ways. Both had taught school, and moved from Mississippi to southeastern Missouri, where school books were free for their son. They were second-hand books from white schools, but their relative value may have been greater than when new.

Very early, he found that his curiosity was aroused by the world around him, and by the classroom. George Washington Carver was a special hero.

Dr. Frederick remembers a Black man name Bruce, who represented the state and who visited Black schools to stimulate interest in agronomy. The students looked forward to Bruce's visits and were impressed that his name was in the encyclopedia, as a phenomenal grower of corn.

The positive recollection of Bruce and his visits is an example of the value of outside stimulus. When life is settled in routine, the arrival of someone new and liked, from a larger world, can be very effective in holding out to the young a prospect or idea larger than had been known before. Bruce represented a larger world, which seemed to be a good and positive world, and within reach.

Dr. Frederick's grade school years, in a one-room school house, were, he now recalls, "a wide exposure." In lower grades, he absorbed knowledge from higher grades, and his knowledge advanced beyond his grade.

In the seventh grade, he took the eighth grade exam for entry into high school, at a time when few even finished the eighth grade. His father was a force behind his progress, and gave his approval to his early taking of the high school entrance exam.

Dr. Frederick took the exam and got the second-highest score in the county. He was just as successful in a run-off examination.

And so he went off to high school in the same general area of southeastern Missouri. Transportation was a problem, but those who want school enough, will find a way to reach it. A converted truck was hired, to be followed by other conveyances when the need arose. The lesson is one not necessarily learned in a classroom. Practical problems must be resolved practically. Transportation was found, contrived, and adapted. And transportation was some-how paid for out of slender means. In 1935, Dr. Frederick's father sent him off to school in St. Louis. High school in St. Louis provided him with his first exposure to regular science. There was the need to adjust to a big-city school; but the teaching quality helped to compensate for any home-sickness.

When the year was over, his parents could not afford to return him to St. Louis; and he went back to the local two-year high school.

There, the scientific interests awakened in St. Louis, intensified. And at home, he began to do drawings of insects to assist in his father's work. Actions and expo-sures were beginning to blend in the direction of science.

In the 6th grade, a new study program was inaugurated for the exceptional student. Dr. Frederick was chosen for advanced training. He spent the summer there and re-calls the condescension and the put-downs from "city folk." At this point, he concentrated on social studies.

At about this time, when he was 13 or 14, one of those events happened which are special, when we look back. Dr. Frederick had been studying the flower, but only in books and in the classroom. One day, while working in his garden, he picked a flower and looked at it. It dawned on him that there in his hand was the object of all his study — the stamens, the pistil, the envelope of petals and sepals, the stem. It was like having read about an exotic place and then going there. It changed his whole outlook on study and career.

When high school was completed, his parents urged that he go to college. He spoke with his fellow students and with his father about the desire to be something. While so many of his fellow students favored Lincoln University in Missouri, Dr. Frederick knew of Tuskegee and applied there.

He was valedictorian, and had received a scholarship to Lincoln; but he held out doggedly for Tuskegee. He was accepted there. He was interested in forestry, agriculture, and taxidermy, but he had then no thought of teaching.

He arrived late for the first quarter and had some early course problems, especially with math. But he recovered all the lost ground, and found that biology and agriculture came especially easy.

Botany caught his interest very early, and a scientific attraction to plants grew. His study of botany became a specialty under a broader heading of Landscape Design. His aptitude attracted the attention of his teachers. He became a teaching assistant, quite naturally, with some real responsibility.

This was the early joining of botany and teaching that was to occupy Dr. Frederick's career. How easily it happened. How fortunate that the man, his superiors, and the subject matter came together to forge a very special life. It needn't have happened, but it did happen; and when it did, he could deliver.

By November, having suffered the loss of his scholarship and a promised job, he had secured a job as a campus night guard. He worked the maximum permissible number of hours and still carried a full academic load. He slept when he could. He says of it: "That was a personal experience."

At the opening of the next school year, he had expected a job as a janitor; but found that the Biology Department had requested him as a biology lab-instructor. Here is one of those critical turns that life takes, in a world of choice and chance. His selection was chance to a degree; but his life to that point had been a series of choices, which made it possible for chance to occur. Almost against his will, he accepted the lab assignment. It worked out well, and he continued in the roll for three years. It was one of many decisive steps in his life.

In contrast to his job as night guard, the lab job permitted more sleep and his grades improved. Nevertheless, Dr. Frederick believes strongly that the obligation to work through college, in moderation, tends to improve a student's academic performance.

His interests while at Tuskegee were very broad. He sought to fill time with useful activities. An enduring interest in journalism established him as Editor of the campus newspaper. Dr. Frederick is a man who would have succeeded in one of several fields. Choice and chance led him to botany.

In the summer following his junior year, he went to work on a tobacco farm in Connecticut, operated by a cigar manufacturer. It was 1942, and it was his first trip out of the South. It was also his first interaction with whites, and with white students as peers. The mind depends upon experience for growth and breadth. Dr. Frederick consistently chose not to stagnate. He liked New England and eventually returned to Rhode Island, for his Master's degree.

At the end of the current summer, he returned to Tuskegee and chose a typically varied and full regimen. He worked for the Campus Digest, with the YMCA, and with civic associations. Stimulated by two outstanding faculty members, he ventured into social activism. One of his mentors had much to do with changing the social face of the South. Forty-five years later, Dr. Frederick is still in touch with this friend and teacher. He seems never to lose a friend.

At the age of 19 (this was in 1943), he graduated from Tuskegee. His determination to go to Tuskegee was matched by his determined harvest of what Tuskegee had to offer. Opportunity is not creation. Opportunity is interaction. It is in the nature of some to extend progressively the limits of growth and experience. Dr. Frederick sought experience, and the growth it offers.

The result can be a blending of mind and spirit, which typifies the unusual life.

Following graduation, Dr. Frederick continued to enlarge his parameters and his potential. He travelled to the Pacific Northwest, and secured an engineering job in the electrical room of a shipyard, where he helped to draft plans for the wiring of aircraft carriers. He remained at the shipyard, doing yet another job well, until November, 1944, when he joined the U.S. Navy.

At boot camp, Dr. Frederick scored very high in language aptitude. When he appeared at the appropriate office for language training evaluation, he was quickly cast aside, literally to the garbage dump. His race was the obvious obstacle. Eventually, he was given training as an electrician's mate and was sent to Hawaii. While he was en route, the atomic bomb fell on Hiroshima and the war was over.

All through his military service, Dr. Frederick pondered his future, and by a process of elimination, focused on botany. His record suggests that he could have been successful in journalism, medicine, architecture, electrical engineering, and biology. Perhaps even linguistics. A variety of options can be as difficult as no choice. Dr. Frederick let time and experience work for him.

In Hawaii, he integrated a Navy drafting room in a manner he now recalls with humor. With little knowledge of architecture, he studied until midnight and, habitually, he came to excel.

He was discharged from the Navy in Hawaii and stayed on at Pearl Harbor, working on naval architecture matters. Already he was taking botany courses at the University of Hawaii, and took Sunday hikes to collect flora. He discovered, in the process, a new species of Hawaiian tree, which is named for him.

During his stay in Hawaii, Dr. Frederick won a considerable circle of close and warm friends in the academic community and elsewhere. Returning there in 1973, 30 years later, he was greeted by them with affection and the honor of a reunion dinner.

In 1948, he began to write to U.S. schools about graduate training in botany, and to think about his botany specialty. He chose plant pathology, and an emphasis on mycology, combining both laboratory and field work. He left Hawaii in August, 1948, and enrolled at the University of Rhode Island. He worked on his Master's Degree, which involved research on Dutch Elm disease.

At the University of Rhode Island, as at other places, Dr. Frederick was blessed with gifted and inspiring teachers who helped to shape his career. He can name four who fit this description, and has molded his own teaching after one who was "a stickler for perfection." He was later to demonstrate his own talent for taking ordinary, even mediocre, candidates and fashioning them into outstanding graduates, whose later careers were impressive.

In August, 1950, he left to undertake work on a Ph.D. at Washington State. It was somewhat familiar territory, because he had spent time in the Pacific Northwest. His thesis was completed in the summer of 1952, and he went to Baton Rouge to teach in the biology department of Southern University.

At Southern University, he innovated by securing a distinct botany program in the biology department, and the establishing of botany as a separate major. He also exposed students to science meetings by simply loading up his car and taking them there.

Dr. Frederick's first botany majors and those that followed were outstanding successes and went on to lives of achievement. His career demonstrates a talent for demanding and eliciting from a student the very best that is in that person. The results are a credit to him and to the students who tried.

In 1962, Dr. Frederick moved from Southern University to Atlanta University, where he was asked to be department chairman, and he remained in that post for 13 years. He dislikes the administrative tasks that come with chairmanships; but with the mark of a true professional, he does them well.

While at Atlanta, Dr. Frederick observed and was involved in racial progress among scientists. In his early years there, segregation problems arose at meetings of the Association of Southeast Biologists. Banquets were cancelled to avoid the seating of Blacks, and there were housing problems at meetings.

In 1963, the first fully desegregated meeting was held, and eventually, he was elected President of both the Georgia Academy of Science and the Association of Southeast Biologists. He also received the Meritorious Teacher Award. He continued to turn out outstanding students and Ph.D candidates.

One Strong Life

Since 1976, Dr. Frederick has been Chairman of the Botany Department at Howard University, in Washington, D.C. He accepted the post on the condition that he could continue to teach. As it is, he performs the roles of teacher, researcher, and administrator. He has no regrets. Twelve hour days are commonplace.

Consider a man who experienced racial discrimination at scientific meetings, in the early 1960's, only to be elected President of the Association a few years later. Such an occurrence speaks of integrity, competence, perseverance, and good will.

Dr. Frederick's life is strong. He sought occasions to grow, and so he was prepared for the things that chance sent his way.

He believes that opportunities come easier for young people as the 20th Century proceeds to its end. Grants, internships, and scholarships are more abundant.

Something's lost and something's gained. Perhaps there are fewer opportunities now to travel the country, working as a night guard, or in tobacco fields and shipyards, or perhaps discovering a new species of plant. It is more difficult now to become acquainted with many lines of work and to learn that one could have done any of them well. Doctor, journalist, electrical engineer, architect, biologist, botanist. Such breadth of experience is a rare opportunity today, as specialization demands an ever narrower focus.

It is the good fortune of education today that persons of Dr. Frederick's abilities and character are teaching the young. Once again, we have a person who over the years touches thousands in ways that are remarkably constructive.

He is singled out for the example of his life, and because he took the time that he did not really have, to share his life with our readers.

Chapter 8

Then and Now

Chapter 8

Then and Now

What has been done, can be done. Blacks can succeed in science, and they can be outstanding scientists. The climate for success is much more congenial now than it was only short decades ago. But it is still not in balance. The glass is half full. If Black Americans are underrepresented in science, they are also represented as never before; and there are steady efforts to increase their representation.

Where we found Benjamin Banneker almost alone in the 18th Century, today we find almost 100,000 Black scientists in the United States. The negative side is that they represent only 2 percent of scientists and engineers in the nation. One solution is to increase the number of Blacks admitted to college, and to encourage their performance while in college. This would increase their employability in science upon graduation from college, or stimulate them to continue their studies in graduate and professional schools.

Statistics that reflect shortcomings are without value, if they generate discouragement and a lack of will to try.

In February, 1989, the National Conference of Black Physics Students met in Washington. The proceedings were described in the Washington Post of February 19, 1989. The article pointed out that an estimated 300 Black physics students in doctoral programs in the USA represented only 2 percent of all physics doctoral candidates. But the conclusion is upbeat: "Knowing that all it takes to help others realize their potential is to care about them, should encourage us all." Progress has been steady from the pre-Civil War period, when Blacks were not allowed to read and write. Moreover, progress has accelerated since the "separate but equal" doctrine was struck down.

The Supreme Court has ruled that public colleges and universities must be desegregated. Before this, only one out of ten Black college or university students was enrolled in a predominantly white college or university. Five years later, seven out of ten Blacks were enrolled in predominantly white institutions.

It is possible to paint a more pessimistic picture of Black progress in science, in both absolute and relative terms. Progress has been slow and progress has been notable. But the Black scientists we have met in preceding pages did not progress with an attitude of pessimism. There is more general encouragement today than ever before. Individual, personal encouragement can come from specific environments, or it can seemingly come from nowhere.

And although solid and continued education is important, more important still is what individuals *do* with the education they receive. There are many successful, respected people with only an 8th grade education, and many college graduates — even those with doctorates — without direction or purpose in their lives, drifting. Black scientists of tomorrow must find an interest, a goal, a passion . . . a dream . . . and believe that there is nothing that will prevent them from achieving that dream. Years of working and attending school — perhaps nights and weekends — are justified by that dream. Others do not have to share in that dream, because it is *yours.*

Optimism is the best foundation on which to plan one's life and nurture one's dreams. A comparison with the past is convincing evidence that there is reason for optimism. As Black students and institutions struggle with the specifics of the day, often in a climate that is ambivalent, they succeed in greater and greater numbers. This trend will continue if only they believe that they can succeed. Optimism is a self-fulfilling attitude.

Even in the face of obstacles put before you by the world, and even concerns or objections from family and friends, dreams can survive. Sometimes the path toward them is circuitous — twisting around poor teachers, turning past jobs and classes that conflict, and winding through forests of responsibilities to family and children — sometimes even stopping for a time when the way seems blocked. But dreams are hardy; they can re-emerge as plants through earth that seemed desolate — surfacing after years when conditions are once again right for their growth. Perhaps they even change, with the education and experiences of their dreamers, and some dreams may not become reality until a second or even third career, but they will persist, as must we all.

It is worth noting that successful Black scientists have come from slavery, from the ghetto, from the big city and the small town, from the farm, from the orphanage, and even the most prestigious families and circumstances. We have democracy within democracy, and a pattern which need not exclude any young person who aspires to a career in science and is willing to establish his or her own path.

Appendix 1

Partial Listing of
Additional Black Scientists

Partial Listing of Additional Black Scientists

Scientist / Year of Birth	Area of Special Interest
A	
Abram, James Baker, Jr./1937	Biology
Abron-Robinson, Lillia Ann/1945	Chemistry
Acker, Daniel R./1910	Chemistry
Alexander, Benjamin Harold/1921	Organic Chemistry
Alexander, Lloyd Ephraim/1902	Biology
Alexander, Winser Edward/1942	Electrical Engineering
Allen, John Henry/1938	Electrical Engineering

Black Scientists of America

Amos, Harold/1919	Bacteriology
Anderson, Charles Edward/1919	Meteorology
Anderson, Everett/1928	Cytology
Anderson, Gloria Long/1938	Organic Chemistry
Anderson, Russell Lloyd/1907	Biology
Antoine, Albert Cornelius/1925	Organic Chemistry
Arrington, Richard, Jr./1934	Zoology
Ashley, William Ford/1920	Chemistry
Atkins, Cyril Fitzgerald/1899	Chemistry
Atwood, Rufus Ballard/1897	Agriculture

B

Baker, Percy Hayes/1906	Zoology
Banks, Floyd Regan, Jr./1913	Physics
Banks, Harvey Washington/1923	Astronomy
Barnes, Robert Percy/1898	Organic Chemistry
Basri, Gibor Broitman/1951	Astrophysiology
Bassett, Emmett/1921	Agriculture

Partial Listing of Additional Black Scientists

Bate, Langston Fairchild/1900 — Chemistry

Bates, Clayton Wilson, Jr./1932 — Electrical Engineering

Baulknight, Charles Wesley, Jr./1911 — Chemistry

Beck, James T./1905 — Chemistry

Bembry, Thomas Henry/1907 — Organic Chemistry

Bharucha-Reid, Albert Turner/1927 — Mathematics

Bias, John Henry/1879 — Biology & Chemistry

Birnie, James Hope/1909 — Physiology

Biship, Alfred A./1924 — Chemical Engineering

Blackwell, David Harold/1919 — Mathematics

Blanchet, Waldo Willie Emerson/1910 — Science Educator

Blanton, John W./1922 — Mechanical Engineering

Bluford, Guion Stewart, Jr./1942 — Aeronautical Engineering

Bluford, John Henry/1876 — Chemistry

Bolden, Theodore Edward/1920 — Dental Pathology

Booker, Walter Monroe/1907 — Biology

Bowie, Walter C./1925 — Veterinary Physiology

Bragg, Robert Henry/1919 — Engineering

Black Scientists of America

Branson, Herman Russell/1914 — Physics

Briscoe, Madison Spencer/1905 — Parasitology

Brothers, Warren Hill/1915 — Mathematics

Brown, Russell Wilfred/1905 — Physiological Bacteriology

Buggs, Charles Wesley/1906 — Medical Bacteriology

Burton, John Frederick/1913 — Forensic Pathology

Butcher, George Hench, Jr./19?? — Mathematics

C

Calloway, Nathaniel Oglesby/1907 — Organic Chemistry

Campbell, Haywood/1934 — Virology

Cannon, Joseph Nevel/1942 — Chemical Engineering

Carruthers, George R./1939 — Astrophysiology

Certaine, Jeremiah/1920 — Mathematics

Chandler, Edward Marion Augustus/1887 — Chemistry

Chappelle, Emmett W./1925 — Biochemistry

Chase, Hyman Yates/1902 — Biology

Chinn, May Edward/1896 — Cancer Research

Partial Listing of Additional Black Scientists

Chisum, Gloria Twine/1930   Experimental Psychology

Christian, John B./1927   Chemical Engineering

Clark, Kenneth Bancroft/1914   Psychology

Clark, Mamie Phipps/1917   Psychology

Clark, Yvonne Young/1929   Mechanical Engineering

Clarke, Wilber Bancroft/1929   Organic Chemistry

Cobb, Jewel Plummer/1924   Cell Biology

Coleman, John William/1929   Molecular Physics

Collins, Margaret Strickland/1922   Zoology

Cooke, Lloyd Miller/1916   Industrial Chemistry

Cotton, Donald/1935   Chemistry

Craig, Suzanne/19??   Mathematics

Crooks, Kenneth Bronstorph M./1905   Parasitology

Crossley, Frank Alphonso/1925   Metallurgical Engineering

Crosthwait, David Nelson, Jr./1898   Mechanical Engineering

Crouch, Hubert Branch/1906   Zoology

Crummie, John H./1936   Electrical Engineering

Crump, Edward Perry/1910   Pediatrics

Cuff, John Reginald/1896	Pathology

D

Dacons, Joseph Carl/1912	Organic Chemistry
Daly, Marie Maynard/1921	Biochemistry
Davis, Toye George/1909	Parasitology
Davis, William Allison/1902	Anthropology
Deese, Dawson Charles/1931	Biochemistry
Derbigny, Irvin Anthony/1900	Chemistry
Diuguid Lincoln I./1917	Organic Chemistry
Donaldson, James Ashley/1941	Mathematics
Dooley, Thomas Price/1904	Genetics
Dorman, Linnaeus Cuthbert/1935	Organic Chemistry
Douglas, Aurelius William, Jr./1934	Metallurgical Eng.
Douglas, William R./19??	Biomedicine
Dove, Ray Allen/1921	Chemistry
Dowdy, William Wallace/1895	Ecology
Drew, Charles Richard/1904	Blood Plasma Research

Partial Listing of Additional Black Scientists

Dorman, Linnaeus Cuthbert/1935	Organic Chemistry
Douglas, Aurelius William, Jr./1934	Metallurgical Eng.
Douglas, William R./19??	Biomedicine
Dove, Ray Allen/1921	Chemistry
Dowdy, William Wallace/1895	Ecology
Drew, Charles Richard/1904	Blood Plasma Research
Dukes, Lamar/1925	Electrical Engineering
Duvalle, Sylvester Howard/1890	Chemistry

E

Edwards, Cecile Hoover/1926	Nutrition
Edwards, Donald Anderson/1905	Physics
Edwards, Robert Valentino/1940	Chemical Engineering
Elders, Minnie Joycelyn/1933	Endocrinology
Eldridge, Henry Madison/1924	Mathematics
Elliot, Irvin Wesley, Jr./1925	Organic Chemistry
Embree, Earl Owen/1924	Mathematics

Ferguson, Angela Dorothea/1925 — Pediatrics

Ferguson, Edward, Jr./1907 — Biology

Ferguson, George Alonzo/1923 — Nuclear Engineering

Finley, Harold Eugene/1905 — Parasitology

Finney, Essex Eugene, Jr./1937 — Agricultural Engineering

Florant, Leroy Frederic/1919 — Mechanical Engineering

Foster, William Clarence/1905 — Physiological Chemistry

Franklin, Hal Addison II/1939 — Cancer Research

Fraser, Thomas Petigru/1902 — Science Educator

Frederick, Lafayette/1923 — Mycology

Fuller, Solomon Carter/1872 — Neurology

G

Gainer, Frank Edward/1938 — Analytical Chemistry

Gibbs, James Albert/1917 — Organic Chemistry

Gier, Joseph Thomas/1910 — Thermal Engineering

Giles, Julian Wheatley/1921 — Otolaryngology

Gipson, Mack, Jr./1931 — Geology

Partial Listing of Additional Black Scientists

Glover, Israel Everett/1913	Mathematics
Gourdine, Meredith C./1929	Physics
Granville, Evelyn Boyd/1924	Mathematics
Green, Harry James, Jr./1911	Chemistry
Greene, Bettye Washington/1935	Physical Chemistry
Greene, Frank S., Jr/1938	Electrical Engineering
Greene, Lionel Oliver, Jr./1948	Neurophysiology
Gregory, Frederick Drew/1941	Astronautics
Griffith, Booker Taliaferro/1905	Biology
Grigsby, Margaret E./1923	Antibiotic Research

H

Hall, Lloyd Augustus/1894	Food Chemistry
Hammond, Benjamin Franklin/1934	Microbiology
Hampton, Delon/1933	Civil Engineering
Hargrave, Charles William/1929	Physics
Harris, Edward Lee/1902	Chemistry
Harris, James Andrew/1932	Nuclear Chemistry

Black Scientists of America

Harris, Mary Styles/1949	Biology
Harris, Wesley Leroy, Sr./1941	Aerospace Engineering
Hawkins, Walter Lincoln/1911	Polymer Chemistry
Hawthorne, Edward William/1921	Physiology
Henderson, James Henry Meriwether/1917	Plant Physiology
Henry, Walter Lester, Jr./1915	Endocrinology
Henry, Warren Elliott/1909	Physics
Higgs, Roland Wellington/1927	Physics
Hill, Carl McClellan/1907	Organic Chemistry
Hill, Henry Aaron/1915	Organic Chemistry
Hill, Mary Elliot/1907	Analytical Chemistry
Hill, Walter Andrew/1946	Agronomy
Hinton, William Augustus/1883	Bacteriology
Hodge, John Edward/1914	Chemistry
Holloman, John Lawrence Sullivan, Jr./1919	Clinical Rsrch
Holly, William G./19??	Chemistry
Howard, Ralph/19??	Chemistry
Hubbard, Philip Gamalieh/1921	Electrical Engineering

Partial Listing of Additional Black Scientists

Hubert, Charles Edward/1918	Anatomy
Hudson, Roy Davage/1930	Pharmacology
Huggins, Kimuel Alonzo/1898	Organic Chemistry
Hunter, John McNeile/1901	Physics

I

Imes, Elmer Samuel/1883	Chemistry
Inge, Frederick Douglas/1896	Plant Physiology

J

Jackson, Richard H./1933	Engineering
Jackson, Shirley Ann/1946	Theoretical Physics
Jason, Robert Stewart/1901	Pathology
Jay, James M./1927	Biology
Jearld, Ambrose, Jr./1944	Zoology
Jeffries, Jasper Brown/1912	Physics
Johnson, Bernard Henry, Jr./1920	Analytical Chemistry
Johnson, Charles E./1939	Microbiology

Black Scientists of America

Johnson, Elgy Sibley/1915	Mathematics
Johnson, Frank Bacchus/1919	Pathology
Johnson, John Beauregard, Jr./1908	Cardiology
Johnson, Katherine G./1918	Physics
Johnson, William Thomas Mitchell/1921	Physical Chemistry
Jones, George Maceo/1900	Civil Engineering
Jones, Howard St. Claire, Jr./1921	Electrical Engineering
Jones, John Leslie/1913	Physical Chemistry
Jones, Leroy/1929	Chemical Research
Jones, Woodrow Harold/1913	Bacteriology
Julian, Percy Lavon/1899	Organic Chemistry
Just, Ernest Everett/1883	Zoology

K

Kildare, Albert Alexander/1897	Physics
King, Calvin Elihaj/1928	Mathematics
King, James, Jr./1933	Chemistry
King, John Wesley/1914	Botany

Partial Listing of Additional Black Scientists

Kittrell, Flemmie Pansy/1904	Nutrition
Knox, Lawrence Howland/1907	Organic Chemistry
Knox, William Jacob, Jr./1904	Surface Chemistry
Koontz, Roscoe L./1922	Radiological Physics

L

Lawson, James Raymond/1915	Physics
Lawson, Katheryn Emanuel/1926	Chemistry
Lee, Charles Bruce/1921	Zoology
Lee, James Sumner/1903	Bacteriology
Lee, James Warren/1909	Protozoology
Leevy, Carroll Moton/1920	Nutrition
Leffall, La Salle Doheney, Jr./1930	Oncology
Lester, William Alexander, Jr./1937	Chemistry
Levert, Francis Edward/1940	Mechanical Engineering
Lewis, Harold Ralph/1931	Plasma Physics
Lewis, James Earl/1931	Electrical Engineering
Lewis, Roscoe Warfield/1920	Animal Nutrition

Lloyd, Ruth Smith/1917 — Anatomy

Logan, Joseph G., Jr./1920 — Physics

Logan, Myra Adele/1908 — Antibiotic Research

Lomax, Eddie, Jr./1923 — Organic Chemistry

Lu Valle, James Ellis/1912 — Physical Chemistry

M

Madison, Shannon L./1927 — Mechanical Engineering

Malone, Huey Perry/1935 — Chemical Engineering

Maloney, Arnold Hamilton/1888 — Pharmacology

Maloney, Kenneth Morgan/1941 — Physical Chemistry

Mapp, Frederick Everett/1910 — Zoology

Marchbanks, Vance Hunter/1905 — Aviation Research

Marsh, Alphonso Howard/1938 — Electrical Engineering

Marshall, Lawrence Marcellus/1910 — Biochemistry

Martin, Alfred, E./1911 — Physics

Mason, Clarence Tyler/1908 — Chemistry

Massey, Walter Eugene/1938 — Theoretical Physics

Partial Listing of Additional Black Scientists

Massie, Samuel Proctor, Jr./1919	Organic Chemistry
McAfee, Leo Cecil, Jr./1945	Electrical Engineering
McAfee, Walter Samuel/1914	Theoretical Physics
McBay, Shirley Mathis/1935	Mathematics
McDaniel, Reuben Roosevelt/1902	Mathematics
McNair, Ronald Erwin/1950	Astronautics
McSwain, Berah Davis/1935	Biophysical Engineering
Mickens, Ronald Elbert/1943	Theoretical Physics
Miller, Russell L., Jr./1939	Cardiovascular Research
Milligan, Dolphus Edward/1928	Chemistry
Mishoe, Luna Isaac/1917	Mathematics
Mitchell, James Winfield/1943	Analytical Chemistry
Monroe, Clarence Lee Edward/1901	Biology
Moore, Ruth Ella/1903	Bacteriology
Morris, Joel M./1944	Electrical Engineering
Morris, Kelso Bronson/1909	Physical Chemistry
Morrison, Harry L./1932	Physics
Moss, Leon Wilson/1937	Mechanical Engineering

Murray, Diane P./19??	Mathematics
Myles, Marion Antoinette Richards/1917	Plant Physiology

N

Nabrit, Samuel Milton/1905	Physiology
Ndefo, Ejike D./1939	Mechanical Engineer
Neal, Homer Alfred/1942	High Energy Physics
Neblett, Richard Flemon/1925	Organic Chemistry
Nelms, Ann T./192?	Mathematics
Nelson, Edward O./1925	Test Engineering

O

Oseni, Hakeem O./1938	Engineering

P

Parker, Charles Stewart/1882	Botany
Parsons, James A./19??	Electrochemistry
Patrick-Yeboah, Jennie R./1949	Chemical Engineering

Partial Listing of Additional Black Scientists

Peery, Benjamin Franklin, Jr./1922	Astronomy
Perry, Rufus Patterson/1903	Organic Chemistry
Phillips, Edward Martin/1935	Chemical Engineering
Pierce, Joseph Alphonso/1902	Mathematics
Pierre, Percy Anthony/1939	Electrical Engineering
Porter, James Hall/1933	Chemical Engineering
Posey, Leroy Raadell, Jr./1915	Physics
Powell, Robert Lee/1923	Physics
Price, Jessie Isabelle/1930	Veterinary Microbiology
Prince, Frank Rodger/1941	Organic Chemistry
Proctor, Charles D./1922	Pharmacology
Proctor, Nathaniel Kipling/1914	Physiology

Q

Quaterman, Lloyd Albert/1918	Nuclear Physics

R

Randolph, Lynwood Parker/1938	Physics

Ransom, Preston Lee/1936	Electrical Engineering
Reed, George W./1920	Nuclear Chemistry
Reed, James Whitfield/1934	Endocrinology
Richard, Howard Mark Simon/1934	Mathematics
Roberts, Erskine G./1919	Engineering
Roberts, Louis W./1913	Physics
Robinson, Lawrence Baylor/1919	Physics
Robinson, William Henry/1900	Mathematical Physics
Rose, Raymond Edward/1926	Aerospace Engineering
Rouse, Carl Albert/1926	Physics
Russell, Edwin Roberts/1913	Chemistry

S

Sampson, Henry Thomas/1934	Nuclear Engineering
Samuels, John Clifton/1924	Electrical Engineering
Sanders, Robert B./1938	Biochemistry
Sayles, James H./1919	Chemistry
Scott, Benjamin Franklin/1922	Radiochemistry

Partial Listing of Additional Black Scientists

Scott, David, Jr./1936	Civil Engineering
Sellers, Phillip A./1919	Nuclear Chemistry
Shabazz, Lonnie/1927	Mathematics
Shaw, Earl/1937	Physics
Sherrod, Theodore Roosevelt/1915	Pharmacology
Shockley, Dolores Cooper/1930	Pharmacology
Simms, Nathan Frank, Jr./1932	Mathematics
Slaton, William H./1910	Chemistry
Slaughter, John Brooks/1934	Physics
Smith, Barnett Frissell/1909	Parasitology
Smith, Robert Wilson, Jr./1918	Mathematics
Smith, Victor Claude/1899	Chemical Engineering
Snead, Jonathan L./1921	Organic Chemistry
Spaulding, Dean Major Franklin/1900	Agronomy
Spaulding, George H./1908	Chemistry
Spellman, Mitchell Wright/1919	Radiation Biology Rsrch
Springer, George/1924	Mathematics
Stancell, Arnold Francis/1936	Chemical Engineering

Stepto, Robert Charles/1920	Obstetrics
Stewart, Albert Clifton/1919	Inorganic Chemistry
Stubblefield, Beauregard/1923	Mathematics
Stubbs, Ulysses Simpson, Jr./1911	Chemistry
Sullivan, Louis W./1933	Hematology
Syphax, Burke/1910	Oncology Research

T

Talbot, Walter Richard/1909	Mathematics
Talley, Thomas Washington/18??	Inorganic Chemistry
Taylor, Julius Henry/1914	Solid State Physics
Taylor, Moddie Daniel/1912	Inorganic Chemistry
Taylor, Welton Ivan/1919	Bacteriology
Taylor, William Charles/1929	Inorganic Chemistry
Terry, Robert James/1922	Zoology
Thaxton, Hubert Mach/1912	Mathematical Physics
Thompson, Emanuel B./1928	Pharmacology
Thornton, Robert Ambrose/1902	Physics

Partial Listing of Additional Black Scientists

Tildon, James Tyson/1931	Biochemistry
Tinch, Robert J./1917	Biochemistry
Tolbert, Margaret Ellen Mayo/1943	Biochemistry
Towns, Myron Bumstead/1910	Physical Chemistry
Trice, Virgil Garnett, Jr./1926	Chemical Engineering
Tulane, Victor Julius/1895	Chemistry
Turner, Charles Henry/1867	Zoology
Turner, Thomas Wyatt/1877	Botany
Tyler, Sylvanus A./1914	Mathematics

U

Urdy, Charles Eugene/1933	Inorganic Chemistry

V

Vay Dyke, Henry Lewis/1903	Organic Chemistry
Vance, Irvin Elmer/1928	Mathematics
Vanderpool, Eustace Arthur/1934	Microbiology
Vaughn, Clarence Benjamin/1928	Oncology

Velez-Rodriguez, Argelia/1936 — Mathematics

W

Wagner, John A./1923 — Biology

Walker, M. Lucius, Jr./1936 — Mechanical Engineering

Walker, Matthew/1906 — Gynecology

Wall, Limas Dunlap/1902 — Parasitology

Wallace, John Howard/1925 — Bacteriology

Wallace, William James Lord/1908 — Physical Chemistry

Ware, Ethan Earl/1900 — Zoology

Washington, Warren Morton/1936 — Meteorology

Watts, Johnnie Hines/1922 — Chemistry

Webb, Arthur Harper/1915 — Biology

Weir, Charles Edward/1911 — Physics

West, Harold Dadford/1904 — Biochemistry

Wheeler, Albert Harold/1915

White, Booker Taliafero W./1907 — Chemistry

Wiley, William Rodney/1931 — Bacteriology

Partial Listing of Additional Black Scientists

Wilkerson, Vernon Alexander/1901	Biochemistry
Wilkins, J. Ernest, Jr./1923	Physics
Wilkins, Raymond Leslie/1925	Organic Chemistry
Wilkins, Roger L./11928	Chemical Physics
Williams, Daniel Adolph, Jr./1924	Physical Chemistry
Williams, Eddie Robert/1945	Mathematics
Williams, Ernest Young/1899	Neuro-Psychiatry
Williams, Joseph Leroy/1906	Zoology
Williams, O.S./1921	Aeronautical Engineering
Williams, Scott Warner/1943	Mathematics
Williams, Theodore Shields/1911	Veterinary Medicine
Wilson, Henry Spence/1902	Inorganic Chemistry
Winston, Hubert Melvin/1948	Chemical Engineering
Woods, Geraldine Pittman/1921	Neuroembryology
Woods, Lloyd Lander/1908	Organic Chemistry
Woolfolk, E. Oscar/1921	Organic Chemistry
Wright, Clarence William/1912	Anatomy
Wright, Jane Cooke/1919	Cancer Research

Wright, Louis Tompkins/1891	Cancer Research

Y

Young, Archie R., II/1928	Physical Chemistry
Young, James Edward/1926	Physics
Young, Moses Wharton/1904	Neuroanatomy

Appendix 2

Bibliography

Bibliography

The Access and Success of Blacks and Hispanics in
    U.S. Graduate and Professional Education. The
    National Academy Press, 1986.

Afro-Americans in Dentistry: Sequence and Conse-
    quence of Events. Dummett, Clifford and Lois, Los
    Angeles: C. Dummett, 1978.

Afro-Americans in Science and Invention. Hayden, Rob-
    ert C., Journal of African Civilization, November,
    1959.

American Negro in the Fields of Science. Haber, Louis,
    September 5, 1966.

The Black American Reference Book. Saythe, Mabel,
    M., Prentice Hall.

Black Journals of the United States. Daniel, Walter. C.,
    Greenwood Press, Westport, Conn., and London,
    England, 1982.

Black Scientists of America

Black Mathematicians and Their Works. Dorrance and Company, 1980.

Black Pioneers of Science and Invention. Haber, Louis, Harcourt, Brace and Wold, Inc., 1970.

Blacks in Science: Astrophysicist to Zoologist. Carwell, Hattie, Exposition Press, 1977.

Blacks in Science and Medicine. Sammons, Vivian Ovelton. Hemisphere Publishing Corporation, 1990.

Century of Black Surgeons. Koshiba, Charles J., and Margaret M., OK Transcript Press, 1987.

Encyclopedia of Black Americans: Edited by W. A. Low and Virgil A. Clift, McGraw an Hill, Inc., 1981.

Famous First Blacks, Alford, Sterling G., Vantage Press, 1974.

The Hidden Contributors: Black Scientists and Inventors in America. Klein, Aaron E., Doubleday and Company, Inc., 1971.

Humanities Doctorates in the United States: 1987 Profile. National Academy Press, 1989.

The Long Memory: The Black Experience in America. Beryr, Mary Frances and Blassingame, John W., Oxford U. Press, 1982.

Bibliography

Minorities: Their Underrepresentation and Career Differentials in Science and Engineering. National Academy Press, 1987.

The Negro Almanac: A Reference Work in the Afro-American. Compiled and Edited by Harry A. Ploski, Ph.D, NYU and Warren Marr II, Editor of the Crisis, official publication of the NAACP, The Bellwether Co., New York, 1976.

Negro Builders and Heros: Benjamin Bravely. University of North Carolina Press, 1937.

The Negro and Scientific Research. Branson, Herman (reprinted from the Negro History Bulletin, April 1952).

The Negro in Science. Taylor, Julius H., Editor. Morgan State College Press, 1955.

Nine Black American Doctors. Hayden, Robert C. and Harris, Jacqueline, Reading, Mass, Addison-Wesley, 1976.

The Path We Tread. Carnegie, Mary Elizabeth. J. B. Lippincott Co., 1986.

Profiles in Black. Innis, Doris Funnye, Core Publications, New York, 1976.

Scientists in the Black Perspective. Young, Herman A. and Barbara H., sponsored by the Lincoln Foundation, 1974.

Black Scientists of America

Summary Report 1987: Doctorate Recipients from United States Universities. National Academy Press, 1989.

Who's Who Among Black Americans, 4th Edition, 1985.

Appendix 3

Index

Index

A

B

Index

C

Index

D

Index

Index

Index

Index

N

O

P

Q

Index

R

S

Index

Index

Y

Z

Books about
African-American
Achievements in History

Black Inventors of America, McKinley Burt Jr., copyright 1969,1989,
ISBN 0-89420-095-X, stock # 296959, $11.95

Black Scientists of America, Richard X. Donovan, copyright 1990,
ISBN 0-89420-265-0, stock # 297000, $10.95

Black Musicians of America, Richard X. Donovan, copyright 1991,
ISBN 0-89420-271-5, stock # 297059, $13.95

Black Americans in Defense of their Nation, Mark R. Salser, copyright 1992,
ISBN 0-89420-272-3, stock # 297130, $14.95

Black Americans in Congress, Mark R. Salser, copyright 1991,
ISBN 0-89420-273-1, stock # 297150, $14.95

Prepay by Check or Money Order:
Include $2.00 per copy for postage ($3.00 for UPS delivery, no PO Boxes)
Quantity orders – call for discounts & shipping charges

VISA, MasterCard, American Express or Discover
Call (800) 827-2499 to order

Purchase Orders:
accepted from Libraries, other Educational institutions and qualified resellers

available from:

National Book Company
PO Box 8795
Portland OR 97207-8795
(503) 228-6345